The Investment of LOVE

by

Clydell White

COLLEGE BOY
PUBLISHING
"We Breed Bestsellers"

SELF HELP/INTERPERSONAL RELATIONSHIPS
MARRIAGE/DATING/CHRISTIAN ADVICE

ISBN-13: 978-1-944110-23-9

Edited by **Armani Valentino**

for College Boy Publishing

Published for print & digital distribution by **Armani Valentino**
Inside Designed & Setup by **Armani Valentino**

Cover Design by **Armani Valentino**

Published in Dallas, TX, by College Boy Publishing. College Boy Publishing is a division of The College Boy Company & ArmaniValentino.com.

Copies of this book may be ordered directly from www.collegeboypublishing.com. Please allow up to 7-10 Business Days for delivery.

The author is available for keynote addresses, workshops, panel discussions, consultations, and radio & television interviews by emailing collegeboypublishing@gmail.com

Printed in the United States of America

08 09 10 11 12 CDAV 5 4 3 2 1

The Investment of LOVE

by

Clydell White

This book is dedicated to my late mother-in-love, Ruthie Mae Murphy. You kept your commitment to your vows, and showed your daughter and I the importance of making The Investment of Love.

The Investment of Love

PREFACE

1. The Investment of Love   1

2. Processes   13

3. To Kill a Ladybug   23

4. Aim for The Head   35

5. Boaz is not the only Man   47

6. Ask For Help   57

7. Men are Cheetah's   71

8. Let Her Leopard   83

9. When Fathers Release Sons   95

10. Dating With A Purpose   107

11. Communicating on Purpose   119

12. Public Front, Private Fun   131

PREFACE

Things have changed, technology is ever advancing, and the culture of our society is a foreign language from the days of an adult's past upbringing. Thus, the days of dating are far beyond sending a handwritten love letter asking someone you think you like, "Do you like me? Please circle yes or no." In fact, the ways we communicate have evolved. Love letters are a thing of the past. The thrill of a steady and patient chase in pursuit of winning the heart of an individual has been robbed by speedy social media inboxing with hopes of expeditiously transitioning into sexting. The sum of these condensed processes usually equal one-night stands filled with mornings of regret.

If you have had this type of experience, you are probably suffering from a reservation to try again. So what do you do? If you're like most people, you block out random people and prevent yourself from giving anyone else you are unfamiliar with a chance. Then, you tell yourself you will only get involved with people you really know or have known for some time. Once putting thought into this, you begin to think and search online for friends from your past, classmates, and old work associates.

Only to discover them now happily married, or interested in genders opposite of your own! Reality sets in that maybe you didn't know them as well as you thought you did. Either way, your biological clock continues to tick as time waits for no one. You then must face the reality that either you are going to take a risk on love again or stay single for the rest of your life. In the chapters to come, I will use my more than 20 years of experience in finding love and building a healthy marriage with my wife of 16 years. Love is definitely an investment. My question for you is, "Are you prepared for the expense?" Let's find out in the chapters to come.

Clydell White

Chapter One

The Investment of LOVE

CHAPTER ONE—The Investment of Love

I'm a firm believer that relationships on earth were strategically designed by God, to directly reflect our relationship with him. Whether healthy or unhealthy, we can better understand how he feels in a relationship with us by how we feel in a relationship with others. Whenever we think of the word investment, we usually think of its parallel with the word risk. Risk is defined as the possibility of loss or injury, with something of VALUE. Anytime we invest in something, we take the risk of losing or being hurt by that in which we invest.

As we look at one of the best investors in history, multi-billionaire Warren Buffet, it causes us to think there is a science to investing without so much risk being involved. Actually, there is, and it's called Calculated Risk. Although still a risk, a calculated risk is a chance taken after careful estimation of the probable outcome. Luke 14:28, "For which of you, intending to build a tower sitteth not down first, and counteth the cost, he have sufficient to finish it?" Even the scripture tells us that if we are going to invest in building something, we must first consider do we have what it takes to finish what we start.

The Investment of Love

Relationships are no exception, as I can't think of a more valuable thing to build with someone in life. We have to be realistic when going into something this important, as to whether or not we have the proper resources, not financially, but emotionally. Are we coming out of a failed relationship because we rushed into it without first having considered? Were we ready to date, or did we seek the first chance at putting our time and effort into something without careful consideration due to the fever of hopeless romantic?

Do not allow your life to be defined by trying to prove to others you're not lonely. Regarding the previous statement that our natural relationships are a reflection of our spiritual relationship with the Father, consider for a moment that you may be having such a hard time with natural relationships because God is having a hard time in a relationship with you. Our communication with earthly relationships could be lacking because maybe we have failed to communicate with the Father. Galatians 6:7 "Be not deceived; God is not mocked: for whatsoever a man soweth, that shall he also reap." This scripture is a direct indication that the withdrawals we receive in life are a result of the deposits we have made. With something as serious as love, stop just taking risks and move towards Calculated Risks.

Let us look to Jesus as the best example related to a calculated risk. The book of Romans 5:8 (NIV) says, "But God demonstrates his love towards us, in that, while we were yet sinners, Christ died for us." Even though we hadn't even accepted him, he played out the scenario and calculated what the future of life would be like with him making the ultimate sacrifice. Because he declared the end result from the beginning of his committed choice, look at where we are today! He made the ultimate investment and is yet reaping a harvest of souls, daily. He was a true visionary who was able to see the potential and possibilities in us before we could even see it in ourselves.

In relationships, like Christ, we must be able to see beyond where a person is at this present time. However, it's a quality many people lack because we expect instant results. Where would we all be if Christ had given up on us?

Understand this one fact; perfect relationships do not exist. The goal should never be a relationship that's perfect, but rather a relationship that's worth it! If you have been in failed relationships, never consider them as losses but rather lessons. If you use the experiences you've had in times past, it is a wealth of knowledge for your future and should shed insight on the things to do and not do.

When you meet someone new, and they tell you about themself with statements such as, "When I love, I love Hard," what they are basically telling you is, "I'm crazy." Steer clear of these individuals because, in most cases, anyone who says these statements are usually a bad investment. Some red flags should be too obvious to miss. Someone who is genuine in any area will never boast of it. Like Nike, they will Just Do It, and demonstrate it through their actions.

Yes, the greatest takeaway about the subject of love is that it's a verb, in which actions should follow. Continued and consistent congruent actions will define the proof of someone's verbal statement of love towards you. Love gives, proven by John 3:16, "For God so loved the world that he GAVE his only begotten Son." Not only will Love give, but it will give its best. The design of men, even from our physical bodies, was designed for us to be givers.

I cannot say I love my wife and kids and never give to them, never provide for them, or never give them my love, attention, and affection. In fact, it is their connection to me that fuels my passion for achieving goals in life to be able to invest in their future. I've learned that if a family doesn't motivate a man to grind in life, nothing will.

You get out of love what you give to love. The New Living Translation of the Bible in Luke 6:38 perfectly defines my statement, "Give, and you will receive. Your gift will return to you in full—pressed down, shaken together to make room for more, running over, and poured into your lap. The amount you give will determine the amount you get back." A relationship cannot reach the height of its potential with individuals who go into it with the mindset of it being 50/50. Both Parties must be willing to invest their best 100/100, only then will you have true fulfillment regarding any outcome that life brings you.

If the relationship fails, you want the peace of knowing you gave it everything you had. If the relationship lasts, you rest well at night knowing you're putting everything on the table. If one survives the other through death, you don't have the guilt of feeling like you could have done more. You never want to be in a "state of questioning" in your mind; Should've, Would've, Could've, and continuously plagued with what if's. Invest so aggressively in love that it warrants the exact return you're looking for each day.

The Investment of Love

Love people so well that it provokes change even within the individual, as Christ did with us, for it was through loving-kindness that he drew us to him. You can literally love the hell out of someone, by being so kind they won't take the chance of being with another. The trap many fall into is thinking that the grass on the other side of the fence is greener. The reality is if you water your grass, it will be green too.

If you're going to invest in love, understand the difference between germination and the time of maturity. Germination is the process by which an organism grows from a seed or a similar structure. Growth begins immediately, but seeing it mature takes time. Love is not about having everything you want, but learning to want what you have.

There has to be a level of peace and contentment you learn to develop about things God gives us, or you will forever run to what you feel is the next latest greatest thing, because it may seem further along than what you have currently. King Solomon stated that the eyes are never satisfied with seeing, meaning that there is always someone that can turn your head for a second look. However, do not allow this to be the bait that causes you to lose focus on what you have spent much time investing.

The ultimate expectation of your time horizon in a relationship should be until natural death. This is the purpose of the vow, "till death do you part." The term time horizon is associated with what's considered a horizon risk. A horizon risk is a risk that is shortened because of an unforeseen event. Even in our careful consideration of entering a relationship as a calculated risk, we do not have a crystal ball that enables us to see all the future events to arise in our lives. For this reason, if marriage is your goal, carefully count up the costs of what the traditional wedding vows state; "I, ___, take **thee**, ___, to be my lawfully wedded husband/wife, to have and to hold, from this day forward, for better, for worse, for richer, for poorer, in sickness and in health, to **love** and to cherish, till death do us part, according to God's **holy** ordinance; and thereto I pledge **thee** my faith [or] pledge myself to you." The vows cover a wide range of possible unforeseen events that should not cause our investment of love to be shortened in an individual.

Just like stocks, a relationship/marriage fluctuates. Some days you're up, some days you're down, there will be good times, and there will be bad times. I speak to you as a man who has been with his current wife for 20 years, dated for two (2), and married for 18 years. I felt the time we have been together was necessary to mention as the society of our timeline has beliefs that marriage is obsolete. Who you listen to for advice regarding what you desire is critical. A person's witness is ineffective when what is preached is not operational in their own life.

The history of our relationship is not for bragging right but rather credibility on the authenticity to teach and mentor this subject to others. It's tough to speak something into the lives of others that is not working in your life. Hebrews 6:12 says, "We do not want you to become lazy, but to imitate those who through faith and patience inherit what has been promised." This passage of scripture is a clear message that we should glean from and pattern ourselves after people who have obtained the promises of God in their lives that we seek in our own.

Although we all have different paths in life we are on, we essentially all desire the same destinations of peace and happiness through healthy relationships in life. There is not an investment that we make in which we are not looking for a return on the investment. Even our Father expects productivity as with the parable of the sowers. Every person has a relationship portfolio, a collection of people in their life, and the entire Portfolio of your relationships in your life should look healthy.

One big mistake people make in natural investing is putting all of their resources in one place. An investment strategy like this works well if you're only looking to gain a return from one source. However, remember we have many relationships in life to balance that all bring us a return in different areas, as different types of love are used to maintain each one.

There are many types of love, but the three (3) main types of love in the Greek cover the majority of relationships in our life. There is Eros Love (sexual, passionate love) for Spouses, Agape Love (Unconditional Love) for Family, Philia Love (Friend Bond) for Friends. If you are blessed with the gift of Living Parents, Siblings, Children, and Good Friends, each of these relationships deserve time and energy in them as they will all give you something different than your Eros relationship can provide.

Because time is limited, we must learn to compartmentalize people in our lives; this helps up to prioritize the needed time in which we can invest. These other relationships are important because if your Eros relationship doesn't last, it is these different relationships that will still be there to carry you through if you have invested in them properly.

Most of the time, it is the relationships of friends, parents, and sometimes even children that you built a relationship with before a spouse ever came into your life. It is a serious red flag to connect with someone in an Eros type relationship that encourages you to disconnect with all other relationships in your life. The correct order of our lives should be God first, family second, and friends third. This order, however, is not to give lesser value to any relationship as each of them is essential in their respective places.

Real friends won't allow you to put them before your family, and real family won't allow themselves to hinder your commitments to God. However, all things must be balanced, and even with your commitment to God, he encourages a healthy family unit and healthy friendships. If he wanted us to stay locked in a room all day praying and speaking only to him, he never would have created these other types of relationships. Keep this in mind and live with balance.

Chapter Two

Processes

I was very fortunate as a teenager to be blessed with amazing parents. By the time I was 16 years old, in 1997, my father had purchased me a brand new 1997 Nissan Altima, off the showroom floor as my first car. Very few of my peers had this luxury at such a young age, but I had yet to understand just how truly blessed I was to receive this type of gift. Upon graduating high school in the year 2000, I was gifted with a second vehicle, a 1997 Mazda 626. I was 18 years old with the title to two (2) vehicles, and still living with my parents at the time.

My father made a deal with me that as long as I went to college and worked, I wouldn't have to pay insurance, maintenance, or fuel expenses. As time went forward, I landed a job at UPS as a truck loader. It started at $10.50 an hour, and as a school kid at 18 years old, it was a good job. Life was good, and I was on the path to a productive future. My wife, who was my girlfriend at the time, was very proud of the start I received and felt secure with her choice on a relationship with me.

After being at the job for a few months, I began to learn of the mandatory process put in place by the company to make it to the level of driving the trucks. That was the

The Investment of Love

dream job everyone desired as it came with pay scales well over 60K + a year with full benefits. It seemed easy to drive a truck around and deliver packages. However, the process of getting to that point was to work eight (8) years for the company as a stocker/loader before being promoted. Stocking the trucks was no easy task. We would easily be spotted running back and forth, checking and grabbing packages coming down a conveyer line, trying to ensure we had the right packages for the correct address. The hours for the stocker/loader job was also not as convenient as driving the trucks in the day time; our shift was from 3:00 AM to 10:00 AM. However, if you could survive the process, you would earn the reward. It definitely gave me a goal to work towards.

Seven months into me being on the job, I began to make the mistake of taking my eyes off my goals and focus on what others had around me. The parking lot at UPS, most days, looked like a foreign auto car dealership. Everywhere I looked, it was a Mercedes, BMW, Lexus, Jaguar, or some other foreign vehicle. I began to lose focus by comparing my process with the process of others.

CHAPTER TWO—Processes

Soon, I gained the worst case of car fever and got a bright idea that I wanted to trade in my cars for a brand new BMW. I rushed home to talk with my father about my brilliant idea. Upon explaining to him what I wanted to do, he looked at me and asked, "Son, is you crazy?" I know that's not proper English, but that was exactly how he said it. He then explained to me that it was a foolish thing at 19 years old, to get rid of two paid for vehicles to take up a car note on a BMW. I told him that if you work at UPS those are the kind of cars you're supposed to drive. But what he tried to get me to realize is that the individuals driving those cars were well established and in their late 30's, 40's, 50's, and 60's. Each of them had gone through the process and earned the right to those types of luxuries in life. He told me that he would not give me the titles to make a decision that would harm me when he had tried to position me for a bright future.

I left the conversation with my dream shattered and heart heavy. I really thought it was the end of the world having two (2) practically brand-new cars paid for that I couldn't trade-in for a four (4) or 5-year payment. Weeks went by, and I even tried to go to my mom and win her vote, only to find her directing me back to my father as a wise mother should. I begged and begged for weeks until my dad finally gave in, so I thought. So, to my surprise my father said, "Ok, I will go to the dealership with you and look at cars, but the condition is that I will only let you trade in one of your cars, and you will be responsible for the car note, the insurance, the maintenance, and the fuel expenses." Without hesitation, I said, "Ok, I'll take it."

We headed to the nearest BMW dealership in Shreveport, Louisiana, and I found a 1998 BMW 325i White with Tan interior with every option fully loaded. We drove the 1997 Mazda 626 as a trade. My father sat down with them and did the deal with ease. I left the dealership feeling like I was on top of the world! I was 19 years old with a practically brand-new BMW! I stopped by my girlfriend's house and picked her up to cruise the town 2 miles an hour so that everybody saw us!

Months went by, and my smiles turned to frowns. Oil changes cost me $125, my car notes were $400, wiper blades were $150, insurance was $100, and that's not to mention fuel expenses for 93 octane gas. What looked easy for others who worked at UPS was becoming a nightmare for me simply because I made the mistake of trying to skip the process.

CHAPTER TWO—Processes

My girlfriend began to call and complain that we no longer went out like we used to, or I no longer bought her things. I was financially drained with the expenses of the car and could no longer live my same lifestyle. I ended up going back to my father asking for help with the costs of the vehicle, and he said, "Surely you don't need help," while reminding me of my statement, "You work for UPS, right?"

The lesson he had tried to teach from the beginning now made sense. What I thought my father said yes to was not yes to a blessing, it was a yes to a lesson. This is why he had wisdom enough to have me keep one of my vehicles and not allow me to trade them both because he knew I would need it again. So, he ended up calling my older sister and selling the car to her to get me from under the note.

My father's intentions were the same intentions of the Father in Luke 15 with the story of the prodigal son. When he gave his son his portion, it was not a mistake because there was more where that came from. The father said yes to teach a lesson, not yes, to give a blessing.

It is only through learning from first-hand experiences that we usually get the lessons our fathers genuinely desire to teach us. Therefore, so it is with God, our heavenly father. He allows some things to happen so we can see why we don't need certain things in life as bad as we think we need them. It isn't because he doesn't desire us to have them, but we are usually asking for them out of season. Paul says it this way in 1 Corinthians 6:12, "All things are lawful unto me, but all things are not expedient." Lawful speaks to permitted, and expedient speaks to something being possibly improper or immoral because it's not convenient or practical. This means that though God allows something, it can be sinful if done in the wrong season. When done in the wrong season, certain actions can cause collateral damage for your life at the time and in the future of which you may not be aware — the best example of this regarding relationships and sex.

Sex was created by God and is lawful, but you only receive the real benefits of it when done in the right season of your life in a marriage. Things such as sex become immoral when not done in the proper season; anyone that truly loves you will not pressure you to do things that are not in season.

Those in relationships of any kind, whether its dating or marriage, don't make the mistake of comparing your beginning to someone else's established history. Follow your process and act accordingly to the season you are in right now. Newlyweds shouldn't focus on the vacations a couple that has been married for 20 years are taking, and try to imitate them. Vacations are lovely, but may not be a good investment for that season of your relationship based on your finances and responsibilities in your household.

Be careful not to compare the person you're with to someone else you see. This is one of the biggest mistakes both young dating couples and married couples make. Be grateful and appreciative of where you are, what you have, and build towards what you desire as it relates to goals. Nothing aggravates a person more than being compared to someone else. It's a dangerous tactic to use in attempts to motivate them into doing what you want. Conversely, it will give you the opposite outcome of what you aim to accomplish.

Never bash what you have as a reality, over what you see as a fantasy! For instance, I try to work out a little bit, and though I may not be as well built as Dwayne "The Rock" Johnson, my wife would have to be a fool to have pictures of him posted up in our house, because the "The Rock" doesn't pay bills at my house, I do. In turn, I would be a complete fool to come home praising Jennifer Lopez for the outfit she rocked on the red carpet and haven't complimented my wife when she is the one who fixes my meals and sleeps with me.

A bird in the hand is better than two in the bush. Don't make the mistake of letting go of what you have to reach for something that you may not ever obtain. One of my mentors taught it this way, love is not having what you want, but learning to want what you have. Stay focused on your process. Appreciate where you are and celebrate where you're going!

Chapter Three

To Kill a Ladybug

CHAPTER THREE—To Kill A Ladybug

At the present age of 37, I'm young enough to relate to millennials but old enough to have been raised old school learning the traditional values of the baby boomers. Growing up in the South, my parents taught me the value of treating people with respect and saying, "Yes, ma'am! No, ma'am! Yes, sir! and No, sir!" It was instilled in me by my parents to respect your elders and never to swear.

Both my mother and father played essential roles in my life towards grooming a gentleman. I saw from my father the consistent work ethic a man must have to provide for his family, and I saw my mother respect, honor him, raise four (4) children, and protect the living he earned. I can remember my mom telling me how to treat and handle a lady, to be kind, and not aggressive.

Every lady desires a gentleman, as every gentleman desires a lady. But, what are the signs of a gentleman, and how do you know the difference when dealing with one? Many men initially start out treating a woman with respect and courtesy. Opening doors for a woman on dates and speaking kindly to her, are things any gentleman will do to gain the interest of a woman. Common sense with any man tells him that there will be no second (2nd) date if he doesn't behave well on the first (1st) date.

The Investment of Love

The newness of anything in life has an initial felling of Utopia. With the purchase of a home, car, or anything one sees that appeals to them, there is a state from the beginning in which everything is perfect. The test to anything you have that determines your love for it is the test time. Time determines how you treat things once they have been in your possession for a while. A new car is always maintained well initially. We tell people upon riding with us, no eating in the car, as we desire to take good care of what we just purchased. In a new house, we will remove our shoes upon entering so that we don't track unwanted dirt and grime onto the floors.

Once the newness of something wears off, the question is how well it is maintained and cared for beyond that point. With natural things, we can trade them in if we no longer like them to upgrade to the newest body style of car or sell our home for the purchase of another one more suitable to our desires. With people, as it relates to relationships, this is not the case. However, some in life go about their relationships the same way; this is the key sign you're not dealing with a gentleman.

The art of a gentleman is a lifestyle and mindset that

a gentleman maintains throughout time. An excellent way to tell how a man will treat a woman is his reaction to how he handles the ladybug, an insect. There is something about the term lady, that causes a true gentleman to handle with special care. From personal experience, I can say not once have I had an encounter with a ladybug and killed it. I can, however, think of countless occasions without hesitation that I've squashed spiders, swatted flies, flushed slugs, and sprayed ants. Something, however, in my mental psyche, will not allow me to mistreat a ladybug even though it's an insect just as some of the other species I've killed. Each time I encounter one, I carefully pick them up and safely release them in the proper atmosphere, delicately handling them with my hands to prevent any harm or danger.

One day while coming back from my lunch break, I saw a ladybug on the inside of my car. After arriving back to work, I carefully got the ladybug to crawl on my hand to remove it from the vehicle, considering that inside the car she may get too hot, or that she may get hungry and couldn't get food.

Once outside my car, I kneeled near grass to release her. An employee noticed me kneeling and could tell I was obviously entertained by something. He walked over and asked, "What are you doing?"

I replied, "Releasing a ladybug. She was inside my car."

He gave me a weird look and said, "Wouldn't it just have been easier to throw it out or kill it? That's what I would do."

Pausing for a moment, I stated, "Dude, that's no way to treat a female. You don't just throw them out. A ladybug must be handled like a lady."

He laughed and said, "It's just a bug, and furthermore, how do you know it is a female? There are male ladybugs as well!"

I told him, "I don't know if it is or not, but I can't take that chance and must treat a potential lady with respect."

We both ended up laughing about the small debate and went our separate ways. I thought I would never even revisit the thought, or even mention it to anyone until one day, an event happened that made me think about it. At work, everyone is well aware that I'm a pastor, and I'm often leaned on and approached by both employees and customers that need advice in different areas of life. For some, it's financial questions. For others, it's challenges that they are having with their children. For the rest, it's relationship issues. No matter the issue, I try to listen to each of them and give sound advice to the best of my knowledge.

This particular time I was approached by an employee than wanted to tell me to pray for someone they knew. They expressed it was a serious issue and that they felt someone's wife might be in physical danger by her husband. Upon listening to them give me the back story on this employee, they began to explain how he's always been abusive to every woman he has been with in the past. It was expressed to me the type of childhood he experienced with having a father that was an alcoholic and abusive towards him.

The only example of how to treat a woman he had was the way he saw his mother treated. As a result, the child grew to become a product of his environment as so many children become. Turns out the individual explaining all of this would finally mention which employee it was that he wanted me to pray for and provide advice on how to move forward with him.

Very little in life catches me by surprise as it relates to how individuals act, or the skeletons that may be in a person's closet. Once he said the man's name, it turns out it was the same individual that called my hand in the past for how carefully I handle ladybugs. At that moment, it was as if I was enlightened about the difference in the mindsets of individuals and how we, as men, view women in general.

It all made sense now as to why it was so disturbing for him to see me care for the ladybug the way I did, especially when mentioning that I thought it was of the female gender due to the subconscious thought because the name lady is involved. Whether the actual insect I handled that day was male or female, it still represented the way the mind of the gentleman thinks as opposed to the average male mindset.

When dealing with males, it's crucial to understand that every male is not a gentleman, and every male is not a man. Some males have not matured to the point to know the value of being chivalrous, courteous, and honorable towards a woman. The thought hit me that there could be more to this ladybug thing than I could have ever imagined. When a gentleman deals with a woman of any kind, he will always handle her gently, whether that woman is his mother, sister, spouse, daughter, or friend. There is just a certain amount of respect warranted by the principle for the female gender.

The first relationship a male has with a female is his mother, and the way he treats and speaks regarding her speaks to how he thinks. It would be wise not to only ask a man about his mother to hear his response, but when meeting her, observe how he interacts with her. When a man views a woman like a gentleman, there will even be a certain amount of respect that he commands towards them. One of the quickest ways to stir the hornets' nest is to make a derogatory remark towards a woman that a man loves. No matter how gentle, he will invoke an immediate mode of defense to protect them at all costs.

Devotion knows no bounds when it comes to the lady a man loves. When a man is raised by a lady, he expects to date and to marry a woman much like her. It is foreign for him not to have the same love from another female that he received from the first relationship with a woman, his mother. A man will treat any lady with respect when she acts like one. Yes, a woman's behavior towards a man will indeed predict how he responds to you. Those that desire respect must carry themselves respectfully. It is foolish to think you can act in a fashion

that is not ladylike and expect to be treated like a lady.

A unique attribute about ladybugs is that they voraciously consume plant-eating insects, and in doing so, they help to protect crops. **The discernment God has given a woman is a defense mechanism built in to warn a man of anything that may cause harm to what he is trying to grow. The promise of God in Malachi 3:11** "I will prevent pests from devouring your crops, and the vines in your fields will not drop their fruit before it is ripe," says the LORD Almighty."

Often, that promise manifests through the protective nature of a woman concerned for the future her man is attempting to build. We, as men, must allow them to serve in this capacity without the intimidation that they are trying to control who comes into your space. Sometimes they can catch a radar reading of someone who is just not right to be involved with during their first encounter of meeting them.

In some cultures, to have a ladybug land on you means the person may then succeed in love, have good weather, experience financial success, or simply receive some other desired wish. Other cultures presume having a ladybug land on you brings good luck, or that whatever a ladybug lands on will be replaced with an improved version. Although these are the fantasy-based beliefs of cultures, it does seem to point symbolically to the scripture of Proverbs 22, "Whoso findeth a wife findeth a good thing and obtaineth favour of the Lord."

The success a man has in life is largely contributed to the woman in his life. With the right lady by our side, we succeed in love, financial success, and have good weather as it relates to our journey being filled with sunny skies emotionally. In 1971 Bill Withers said it this way, "Ain't no sunshine when she's gone, It's not warm when she's away." This song speaks volumes on what the presence of a woman in a man's life does for him. When a man is blessed to find a wife as the lady of his life, how he treats her is directly connected to how God responds to his prayers. This is supported by scripture in1 Peter 3:7 (NIV), "Husbands, in the same way, be considerate as you live with your wives, and treat them with respect as the weaker partner and as heirs with you of the gracious gift of life so that nothing will hinder your prayers."

To kill a Ladybug naturally speaks to the way a man thinks towards a woman. However, to purposely mistreat a woman is to Kill a Ladybug spiritually, which in terms can kill your influence with others and hinder your progress with God!

Chapter Four

Aim for the Head

CHAPTER FOUR—Aim For The Head

As it relates to relationships, many are faced with the thought of "What should be the focus." I've learned men and women like what they like as it relates to the qualities that they find attractive in others. I do believe wholeheartedly we can have true love and enjoy the qualities of what we are attracted to in another. The problem with being solely driven towards what we are attracted to is that we become temporarily blinded by our present wants and don't consider our future needs.

No matter what your present age is, the key to success in choosing wisely in relationships is always to consider the future years beyond where you are. If you're 20, you want to ask yourself, "What will I need in my 30's and 40's, etc.?" Too often, people make the mistake of going after what they see now because it appeals to them physically. However, as the years pass, they often find themselves growing apart because the person lacked the qualities that would be vital through the transition of the many changes, we as adults go through.

Men are often the worst at not knowing what they need, they just know what they want, and there is a vast difference between the two. God's promise to us in Philippians 4:19, "But my God shall supply all your need according to his riches in glory by Christ Jesus," was never based on wants. It is based on supplying our needs.

Many times, God has provided us the one we will need in life, but we often miss it because our focus is only on what we think they should look like physically. As a man myself, I can speak for the changes a man goes through with every decade of his life, at 37 years old now, my mind is far different about what I want from a marriage than it was when I was 21.

My wife has been exactly what I needed through every stage and phase I've gone through. Women are tasked with the challenge of transitioning and adapting quickly to the seasons of a man's life. In 1978, a chart-topping song was written by Nickolas Ashford and Valerie Simpson titled "I'm every woman." Legendary singer Chaka Khan would be the voice to bring this classic to life, and it would go on to be a remake from the late great award-winning songstress, Whitney Houston. The subject matter and lyrics accurately describe the personality a woman must have in dealing with a man. The song states, "Whatever you want, whatever you need; Anything you want to done, baby, I'll do it naturally; Cause I'm every woman (every woman) It's all in me, it's all in me, yeah!"

A woman cannot be a one-trick pony and intend to survive with the man she plans to grow with, as she will encounter and see many changes in him with each decade that passes in his life. Men are almost like the dog who chases a car. Once the car stops and they catch up with it, they don't know what to do next. Some men just enjoy the chasing of women and the sport that comes along with it.

Our purpose for pursuing a relationship in life cannot be left to chance. We must be intentional in what we invest our time in, as time is the most valuable source we have. Money and things can be replaced if lost, but time can never be regained. With this in mind, it behooves us not to waste it.

Pop culture has been a very negative influence on those with hopes of building a lasting relationship. Regarding men, the method for connecting with women has been reduced to owning impressive possessions to be a magnet to attract them. Society makes you think you must have the best car, the biggest house, or the most uber attire for women to gain interest in you. Even the music of the culture has changed. It went from the love ballads to stunt music that focuses on who can spend the most money in the club.

Marketing schemes for this type of behavior are well thought out because the industry knows for this generation, sex sells. This, however, is not a lifestyle that is conducive to having a serious, committed, and mature relationship. Women who have their heads on straight are not impressed by any of these tangible things. Most of the time, they own all of the same toys men own themselves.

There are, however, those of the female gender who can be shallow enough to fall for the flamboyant lifestyles of men who flaunt trinkets for tricks. The result of these thrills leads to emptiness and unfulfillment. Either way, no matter how successful a woman is, there is yet a void that only the presence of a man can satisfy.

But for both men and women, my focus with this chapter is to get you to adjust your aim because if your goal is only on what's below the other individual's core, you will never be able to have enough of it to find true satisfaction. There is more to life than lips, hips, and fingertips, as these alone will not quench a man's desire. Let us consider a wise King, Solomon; Ecclesiastes 1:14 says, "I have seen all the works that are done under the sun; and, behold, all *is* vanity and vexation of spirit."

Upon my studying of this statement, we find that the King was depressed. Yes, you can indeed have money, things, power, women, and still, be depressed. Contrary to the image pop culture paints, the accumulation of things, and having plenty of men or women at your disposal does not make us happy. Here is a man who states in the chapters of Ecclesiastes that his attempts to find happiness in every activity possible, were all vanity. He built cities. He planted a diversity of trees. He withheld not his indulgence towards anything his eyes saw. He had 700 wives and 300 concubines totaling a thousand women and still couldn't find satisfaction. His life was constantly focused on trying to have a good time to try and find peace, and it was to no avail when he finally realized the rich man had to die just like the poor man.

This caused him to say about life, that it's all vanity. Solomon was the result of a generational curse. His father, the previous king, King David, fathered him as the result of taking his mother, Bathsheba, from her husband Uriah by having him sent to the front lines to be killed in battle so that he could have her. What sparked his interest in her initially is because of how he saw her on the rooftop, bathing.

When you're driven solely by the physical, you will stop at no boundaries to try and satisfy yourself with what you are attracted to. Proverbs 27:20 says, "Hell and destruction are never full; so the eyes of man are never satisfied." Since King David did not deal with this issue correctly, his son Solomon fell victim to the same struggle 999 times more, literally.

What you fail to deal with in one generation will be magnified in the next generation. It is our duty to teach our sons and daughters the power of connecting with someone on a mental and emotional level. It's a truth that a large percentage of people in marriages and relationships still have minds that are connected with someone else. This happens as a result of not aiming to fall in love with the mind of an individual.

Even in our efforts to maintain our appearances and physiques, and everything about our natural beings are temporal. At some point, the six-pack for men will become one-pack, and the features of a woman will sag. If we have not fallen in love with an individual mentally, nothing physical about them will be enough in itself to ever satisfy us.

CHAPTER FOUR—Aim For The Head

No measurements will ever be good enough, no job will ever earn enough, and no house will ever be big enough. People get married for lots of reasons that are not always the right reason. For some, it's a convenience and financial security. For others, it's a cover-up to stay in right standings with a certain social status. For some, it's just to have legal sex that is classified as fornication. All of these are the wrong reason and usually result in them being with a person to fill the direct need, but the whole they are with someone else who reaches them on an emotional level.

The emotional connection with someone is far more powerful than any physical connection you can have, as it is a spiritual connection. Though a person may not physically be present with someone, the bond they have mentally will keep them knitted in ways a touch can't. It's the essence and ingredient that has kept individuals happily together even when health challenges are faced that prevents physical intimacy. There is yet a mental intimacy that brings fulfillment to one another.

If you are reading this and you're in a relationship, you want the comfort of knowing you're with someone present both physically and emotionally. Many are in bed physi-

The Investment of Love

cally each night with someone who is mentally sleeping with someone else, or with someone whose heart belongs to someone else.

I stand as a witness that when dealing with women, there is no higher form of lovemaking than when a man can make love to a woman's mind. The ability that a woman has to think the way she does is a benefit to a man. Don't be fooled by the stories of secular artists advising men to "beat it up" as it relates to intimacy, as no woman wants that type of experience. The anatomy of a woman is considerably different than that of a man; pleasure for women is not experienced in the same fashion as men. I can guarantee, though, the man who masters mental intimacy with the woman in his life will never want for anything as it relates to his satisfaction.

Aiming for the head of an individual will produce moments in time that will become the best memories of your life with one another. As you grow together in both bond and age, it will be these memories you have to look back on together that will go beyond the limits of your physical possibilities. It is not realistic to have physical pleasure every day and moment of your life, but you can have mental pleasure from the joy you bring each other emotionally.

Imagination can take you to places mentally. Use your imagination to create new ways to please and surprise one another. The majority of what happens to us in life is more mental than it is anything else anyway. If you can build from your imagination, you can have it in the physical or real -life as the young folks say.

When you have an emotional support system in your lover that is secure, there is no storm you cannot weather, no hill you cannot climb, and no valley you cannot endure. God created man to have joy spiritually, mentally, and physically. He designed us with all of these areas in mind. I admonish you if you are in the phase of dating or a serious relationship; to experience pure bliss, shift your focus to aiming for what truly matters; The Head/Mind of an individual.

Chapter Five

BOAZ
is not the
Only Man

CHAPTER FIVE—BOAZ is NOT the Only Man

The most famed story in the Bible as it relates to women being awarded their knight in shining armor is the Story of Ruth and Boaz. While many women celebrate this story and use it as a model while "Waiting for your Boaz," I do not want you to limit your hopes on being found by this type of individual only. As Boaz man represents only one type of man. Many women admire the qualities of Boaz because of the level of financial security and stability that he provides. While those are indeed great qualities to have in any man, those are not always the only qualities a woman needs for the season of life she is in currently. While it is understandable to desire for God to send a man with the status of Boaz, women must think more realistically as to whether their qualities fit the qualities of Ruth. It's one dimensional to desire a man to meet certain criteria in life, without also thinking accountably about holding yourself to the same standards. What if the Boaz type of man you're waiting to find you, is looking for a Ruth with the exact circumstances of what he reads of her to be in the Bible? What if he is erroneously grooming himself to think one dimensional that the only woman he seeks for should have the direct attributes and circumstances of Ruth.

The Investment of Love

Take a moment to ask yourself an honest question as to whether or not Ruth's situation lines up with yours? Ruth, for instance, didn't have children with her first husband, Mahlon. Having no children is a very rare scenario for many marriages that end in death or end because of divorce. So if you're looking for someone with qualities of Boaz, in turn, they may be looking for someone whose situation is along the lines of Ruth, as this is a reality that some men are turned off by connecting with someone who has kids.

Ruth also had so much love and endearment for her mother-in-law that even after the death of her husband, that she refused to leave her mother-in-law and followed her. She had a strong connection and trusted her. Some women cut off all communication with their mother-in-law while married to the woman's son. Even more of them do so after a relationship with their husband dissolves.

So, if you base your dreams solely on one type of story in the Bible to hope for, you would be disqualified if you didn't meet the circumstances Ruth also met. We must, therefore, begin to draw strength from scriptures that are a fit for our direct circumstances in life. One of the main revelations to take away from the story of Ruth and Boaz is the reality it's possible to lose a relationship and start again. One can gain hope from the story of Ruth that regardless of how your previous marriage or relationship ended --- whether by the death of a spouse or the love of the relationship simply died, causing you to grow further apart --- God is able to position you in the proper circumstances to encounter the person you can spend the rest of your life with, in peace.

As I stated earlier, there are many individuals with qualities that are essential for maintaining a healthy relationship once you are considering making the investment of love, again.

There is another story that comes to mind that represents another type of man who could be near you, but your focus on expecting a Boaz has blinded you from seeing him. That man is Joseph, and he represents a type of man that most women overlook. What is so special or powerful about Joseph, you might ask? Let's find out and focus on Matthew 1:18 where it says, "This is how the birth of Jesus the Messiah came about[a]: His mother Mary was pledged to be married to Joseph, but before they came together, she was found to be pregnant through the Holy Spirit." Can you imagine coming home to the man you're engaged to be married to and have to explain to him that you're pregnant by someone else? Although that other person in Mary's case was The Holy Spirit, you understand my point I'm making.

Can you imagine how farfetched that would sound to a man to hear that statement from the woman he's taken home to meet his mother and told all of his close friends he was going to marry? Joseph had a quality of obviously being very understanding, and his response showed us he was not one to be physically violent after what Mary told him.

If any scenario had brought out the absolute worst in Joseph and expose his true character, it would definitely have been him receiving this news. An outstanding quality you find in a Joseph is peace. One of the most disheartening things is to be involved and connect with someone abusive towards you. It makes it difficult to have real peace of mind while always living on pins and needles with someone. A man filled with anger can't even work productively in society without being consumed with rage. Yes, there are a lot of men that may have the wealth of Boaz and can provide for you, but what good is money if they don't provide peace towards you. You will never be able to enjoy the financial security for a lack of a man's emotional stability towards you.

CHAPTER FIVE—BOAZ is NOT the Only Man

Look at what Joseph does next in Matthew 1:19, "Because Joseph her husband was faithful to the law, and yet did not want to expose her to public disgrace, he had in mind to divorce her quietly." Joseph also had the quality of obeying the law and is even mentioned as being faithful to it. When you are faithful to something, it is a reflection of your real character. When you're a person of good character, even when people are not around to witness your behavior, you will still uphold what you know is right. This is a quality that is both spiritual and natural.

Faithful people can be trusted, and if you have ever been involved with a man you couldn't trust, then you should be rejoicing at the fact that some Josephs still exist that can be trusted to do what's right even when you aren't looking. It has been said that character is who you are, even when no one is around watching you. Half of a woman's emotional stress from a failed relationship involving infidelity is the trust issues that come with her trying to move forward with someone new.

The peace of mind that comes with trust can more than compensate for the lack of how rich a man is, he may not have wealth, but he won't give you worry. Even Joseph heard this news from Mary; he didn't get upset. The Bible points out that he had planned to divorce her, and we must with understanding see his reason as to why, because that is more than any other individual male or female can endure. Being a man that is faithful to the law, those are grounds for calling the engagement and marriage off.

Another quality to consider about his character is he planned to do it privately without publicly embarrassing her. This proves Joseph was not messy. In today's time, he would not have taken to public platforms such as social media to air out what you told him in confidence. Anyone who does not have proper social media etiquette should be a red flag to you. You can tell a lot by viewing someone's social media pages. It's a free background check on their behavior, so start studying the social media pages of an individual before falling head over heels into a relationship with them. Their page may tell you a lot about how confidential a person is by how they Live out Loud in public.

As we look deeper into the story of Mary and Joseph in Matthew 1:20-21 it states, "But after he had considered this, an angel of the Lord appeared to him in a dream and said, Joseph son of David, do not be afraid to take Mary home as your wife, because what is conceived in her is from the Holy Spirit. 20 She will give birth to a son, and you are to give him the name Jesus because he will save his people from their sins."

Joseph obeyed the voice of God and did exactly as God instructed him. Ladies, it is crucial to understand that when dealing with a Joseph, through misunderstandings that even when you can't get through to him, God can! Sometimes there will be things that you can argue and explain to a man that he will never get when you are birthing something spiritually. However, when a man has a relationship with God, the Lord will confirm some things to him to endorse and back what you have said in conversation to him. As the man, being the head of the house, it is not your job to overrule his God-given place. But, you can take comfort in knowing that when something is of God, he will always reveal it to the man.

Lastly, the reason Joseph shined on the level of a Boaz is that Joseph will accept, father, and provide for a child that he didn't produce. This is good news for a woman who may have children by another man, a woman whose relationship didn't work out, or was widowed but has a child or children.

The Investment of Love

God has some Josephs out there who will love your son or daughter as his own. It takes a special man to do that, and these men should be celebrated.

A woman limits herself when waiting for her Boaz when your situation is more realistic for a Joseph. Never put God in a box as to the kind of man he wants to send into your life. Although you may have your wish list, God's will provides what he knows we need. Trust his plan for your life, and keep an open mind as it relates to the men around you. Many times the one that's right for you is closer than you think.

Adjust your focus towards the qualities that are going to matter in the long run. Peace, Love, Joy, Trust, and Happiness are all things no amount of money can buy. They are given from God and must come from within the man. The key to your fairytale ending may be as simple as giving Joseph a try, knowing that you can still live happily ever after!

Chapter Six

ASK
for
Help

One Saturday morning at home, my wife and I, while finishing breakfast, noticed the garbage disposal wasn't working. Water had backed up into the opposite side of the sink. After observing for a moment, I figured it had to be a clog of some sort between the pipes underneath the sink. I've never had any plumbing experience, but I thought to myself, how hard could something like this be? It was a weekend, so the chance of getting a professional to come out at the last minute was not realistic.

I decided to do what most millennials would do and YouTube the issue. Several videos came up in my search, and the first one I saw was with a single woman fixing her plumbing as a first-timer by herself. That gave me hope as a man because I thought to myself, "If she can do it, I can do it too." Whether that way of thinking was right or wrong at the time, it's still transparently what I had thought.

I didn't tell my wife I was looking at YouTube for the fix and dare didn't show her the video of a woman doing it, so that if I tried, and it didn't work she wouldn't be able to tease me by saying, "A woman did it, and you can't!" Instead, all I did was tell her, "I can't get a plumber on a Saturday. So, I will fix it myself."

She looked at me, surprised, and said, "What? You're going to fix it, oh ok."

Giving her the side-eye, I said, "Just wait. I'll have it back up in no time."

Fortunately, it was a free Saturday, and I didn't have any obligations for the day and could focus solely on this. I went and got my toolbox and dressed appropriately, sitting everything near the kitchen sink. I only needed to see the YouTube video once, as it was pretty clear and basic what was described to me to do. I opened up the bottom drawers of the sink with high hopes on what the outcome would be. I detached first the pipe that connected from the garbage disposal to the opposite side of the sink.

Upon loosening it, the excess water started to drain. However, I was already prepared and had a bucket to catch the water. Once I got the pipe loose and looked in it, I saw a massive build-up of grease that was causing a blockage in the pipe. I then cleaned all of the build-up out and began to take apart the other pipes to check them as well. Each of the pipes had the same problem, and I treated each of them accordingly.

So far, this was all seeming like an easy fix; I then

began to reattach all of the necessary fittings and pipes to give the sink a try to determine if it was repaired. Once it was all reconnected, I stood up for the moment of truth, lifting the sink handle on the spout, and water began to flow. I stepped back to observe with the cabinets open, that everything was tight and that there were no leaks.

Water ran for minutes without a single hiccup. I then started the garbage disposal to make sure it was also working correctly while the water was running. I had a huge sigh of relief, and a great sense of pride that I was able to fix the problem was a blessing on many levels, and it saved us money.

I hollered my wife's name, and she came into the kitchen, wondering what the loud shout was about. I told her, "I fixed the problem."

She lit up with joy and gave me a high five. Then, she asked me, "What was the problem, and how did you fix it?"

I explained, "It really wasn't much to it." in a very confident tone.

She told me, "You're awesome and can do anything!"

The Investment of Love

The affirmation I received alone from that statement was worth every moment spent doing the job. Nothing makes a man feel more special than when he is looked up to as the fixer of things in a household.

Months and months went by, and the sink operated properly without any issues. Another random day our kids suggested instead of eating out for my wife to do a taco bar and make them at home, as she makes the best tacos and guacamole. She made a trip to the market to get all of the necessary ingredients to prepare the meal.

When she cooks, she always makes more than enough to feed almost twice the size of our family, that's just kind of her thing that she does. I never make a fuss of it because it's always been that way. In marriage, you learn over time to pick your battles, and that is not one worth fighting, so we just go with it.

Everyone had finished eating for the evening, and I went about my normal routine of going into the bedroom to play videogames for a bit. I was in the middle of a boss fight on a game I was playing and overheard my wife say from the kitchen, "The sink is not draining." Now, of course, I tried to act as if I didn't hear her because I didn't want to be pulled away from my current focus on the game I was playing. So, I continued to play.

Finally, she came into the room and said, "Clyde, the sink is stopped up again!" At that point, I got up to go and see what the issue was, and upon looking at the problem, it seemed to be just like the last. There was something clogged between the pipes. I thought for a moment, though the build-up could not be that bad this soon from the pipes as it was thoroughly cleaned out the last time, just a few months ago. So, I then begin to ask my wife when exactly did she notice the problem and what happened? She then told me she was disposing of the black beans as much was leftover. Instantly, I knew that if she attempted to put that many black beans in the garbage disposal that it could possibly be the issue. I didn't fuss, I just stated, "Give me a second, and I'll fix it.

I thought back on my last repair and figured I would do what I knew how to do, and it would be back up and running. Repeating all my same steps, I went through the same routine of getting my tools and clothing sitting them by the sink. The only difference is this was a weekday night and not a Saturday morning. I didn't have any obligations, but having already worked a full day, getting off at 5:00 pm, and having to prepare for work the next morning, made me feel some way about being underneath the sink. I normally try to be in bed by a certain time. Fortunately, though, the last time I made this repair, it was done in less than an hour, but going into it this time knowing what to expect, I could do it in less time than that.

Once I took off the pipes underneath the sink, the water mixed with black beans begin to pour. I took a bucket full of black beans and water and dumped it out. Coming back to clean the pipes out I was breezing through the process, upon cleaning them all out, I reattached everything and started the water, backing up to observe underneath the sink I saw no signs of leaks. However, once I looked back into the sink, I saw that the water wasn't going down.

I stopped the water and thought for a moment. I knew for a fact I had cleaned out the pipes well and reconnected everything just as I did the last time that I fixed the problem. I cut on the garbage disposal to see if it would push through anything trapped on its side, and yet the water still did not clear. I didn't panic and just decided to disconnect the pipes again to be sure they were clear and clean. Just as I thought I cleaned the pipes properly and nothing was trapped between them, I reconnected everything hoping it would work right this time. Still, it was to no avail on being fixed.

I started looking up on YouTube to see what could be the problem. My wife came in the kitchen, having noticed I was in there this time longer than the last time and asked, "Did you fix it?" She meant no harm in her asking the question, but I responded, "No" in a tone that was out of frustration. I had already worked that day and was way past going to sleep at my normal bedtime, and would still need to shower from trying to make this repair.

She could tell I was frustrated and begin to apologize for putting the beans down the drain, upon hearing that I didn't want to make things worse and I said softer, "It's ok. I will figure it out."

She said, "Ok," and went back to the bedroom to give me space to do the job. I went back and forth on trying things and discovered the problem was terrible this time. The water in the dishwasher was backed up as well, from opening it to check water it had poured out onto the floor, which was another problem because now I would have to clean that up and mop as well and yet the problem still hadn't been fixed.

The Investment of Love

I had now been working on this for well over 2 hours. My wife came back in to offer me something to drink, which was the sweetest gesture and immediately diffused some of my frustration. She looked at me and could tell I was tired physically and mentally, stated softly, "Clyde, just come to bed and call the plumbers in the morning." Hearing that gave me mixed emotions, as part of me knew that was the best option, the pride I had as a man egotistically caused me to want to fix our problem myself as opposed to someone coming in and doing it for me.

A man is disturbed by not being able to fix something, especially when he has done it before. I like to be viewed as the fixer of things for my family, and it's damaging to a male ego when he can't be viewed in that regard.

Still having too much pride to listen to my wife on getting a professional involved, I told her I wanted to try one more thing. Once she left again to the bedroom, I called a personal friend of mine who is experienced with plumbing work to see if he could guide me through what to do. I explained to him the exact scenario, and he asked me if I had a snake tool, because the root cause of the problem was not related to what was on the surface of what I could see.

The problem was much deeper, and I would have to be able to reach the blockage, which could be as far as 25 feet away from where I could reach.

His advice was to get someone professional involved that does this for a living and to trust them as the expert to help correct the problem. Finally, I yielded for the night and went to bed, admitting to my wife that I would get professional help in the morning. The next day I scheduled an appointment for the same day for someone to come out and fix the problem.

When the professionals showed up, they had us back up and running in no time, and used the snake tool my friend had mentioned because our problem was much deeper than what I was able to reach with my own abilities.

There is a valuable lesson in this story as to why I was led to share it with you. In relationships, sometimes we have problems in our household that are deeper than we are able to work out amongst ourselves. Growing up in a faith-based family, we are taught when having an issue to just pray about it, and everything would be alright.

The idea of going to professional counseling and therapists to deal with deeper issues is often frowned upon.

The Investment of Love

We somehow feel it devalues our faith in the immortal if we seek someone mortal to settle our differences.

We must remember that even the people placed on this earth that help and assist us are still ordained of God, and have their place. It is God that has given the intellect and knowledge to professionals to handle natural problems just as he gives the intellect and revelation to ministers who handle spiritual issues. Everything in life is not always a spiritual/religious issue, and our failure sometimes can be as simple as us having too much pride to seek counsel because our ego wants us to be seen as perfect. I'm not saying with every issue run to someone else to solve and settle your matters, but there may be problems that arise in which you are personally unable to resolve.

Too many people give up without having exhausted every option of trying to fix the problem. In our case, what sense would it have made to leave the house and get a new one just because I didn't want to deal with the problem we were having with our plumbing? After investing so much to make that our place of refuge and peace, it would be crazy to get a new home over something easily solved by a professional plumber.

Your relationships in life deserve that same way of thinking, you have invested too much into them to replace them with someone new just because you have too much pride to sit down with someone who can help you. If you are reading this on the verge of throwing in the towel, I want you to consider my advice and seek someone professional to help. The person you will find to help in this matter will not always be a member of your church or your church's clergy.

Consider a neutral source so that neither person involved will feel that the mediator is biased and that both sides are heard without favoritism. In the event, things still don't work, then cross that bridge when you get there. However, you will live with a considerable amount of regret continually asking yourself the question, "What if we had tried professional counseling?" If you did not make that conscious effort, don't be guilty of letting your pride prevent your peace.

Chapter Seven

Real Men are Cheetahs

CHAPTER SEVEN—Real Men are Cheetahs

In an attempt to help women understand the male race, we are a lot like cheetahs from the animal kingdom! If you're saying within yourself, "I know that's right," let me assure you I didn't say, "Cheaters." So, before you high-five me, please don't confuse any bad experiences you may have had with men in terms of what I'm referencing here.

One day while I was preparing for a sermon series, I did research and studied different cats in the animal kingdom as hunters. My findings regarding the cheetah were fascinating; most only know them as the fastest land animal reaching sprint speeds of 60 to 70 mph. They are known to live in a variety of environments, including dry forests, grasslands, open plains, and deserts.

They are not hiding, or as rare of a site as some may think, all you have to do is look around you. Do you ever feel like you are in a dry season from the lack of long-term male candidates like the dry forest provoking a variety of adaptations to your life to accommodate your singleness? Maybe you feel like you're living in the grasslands, an area where the vegetation is dominated by grass because it seems to be overpopulated by women, and under populated by men. Cheetahs in the open plains are probably the toughest though to grasp because how could something that phenomenal of a specimen be in plain sight?

The truth is the best place to hide something is in the open because most will never look for it there, as that seems too practical. Then there are deserts, barren areas where little precipitation occurs, and conditions seem to hostile for animal life. Why would cheetahs want to be there, where there is not much to offer them, in exposed areas that can't provide protected surfaces? Surely, they are not interested in being there. Fortunately, for Cheetahs, these large felines do not need much water to survive, and they get most of what they need while eating.

With this being said, they are not the opportunists' people might think. Cheetahs are where they are because that's where they want to be; they can survive anywhere they chose to and are not worried about the conditions they have to endure.

Have you been wondering where the men are? I challenge you to open your eyes and realize that there are good men still, everywhere. Forgive yourself of thinking that your habitat is too strenuous for a man to find interest in it, or that there are no men in your city, your career field, or your church. That is a mindset far from the truth.

If there is one thing about cheetahs of the wild, you need to know what will give you the advantage of having a healthy relationship with men is this: They only eat fast food! One of the biggest issues with the relationships of this generation is retention. Connecting with someone new seems to be easier than holding their interest for an extended period these days.

Society has shaped a desire for instant gratification in more ways than one. Subtly, through the years, dial-up internet has changed to high-speed internet, with engineers continuing to push the limits of upload and download speeds, while cellular companies have tapped into 5G speeds for consumers. This is indirectly training the minds of people to have what they want without any delays. So, this is generally the mistake most women make without even consciously thinking about is being Too Fast! But wait!!! I know you're confused. You're probably thinking, "I thought you said cheetahs only eat fast food." Yes, you are correct. That's exactly what I said. Follow me closely, as I explain.

In my research on cheetahs, I've found they do not like to be fed. They enjoy the hunt of Gazelles and Impalas.

The Investment of Love

Both of these are land animals with capabilities of sprinting 50 to 60 mph, causing the enjoyment and thrill of pursuing something that challenges their natural abilities of speed. You will never find a cheetah going after a turtle. It's too easy and requires no challenge. Therefore, Cheetahs only desire fast food and are fueled by the challenge of pursuing its prey.

In similar terms, any man truly worth building with doesn't want you to be easy. He desires the challenge of winning your heart. Be the type of catch that requires a man to think. Be creative and keep his interest by going at a steady pace in newly formed relationships! Men are not as shallow as women claim them to be unless these women were used to entertaining boys.

A real man is the opposite, and desires the lady of his life to have morals and values! If you have been providing your man's food and shelter, this is no long-term benefit to you and causes more harm than good to him. You will know you are dealing with a cheetah in your life by having a man that desires to go out and make provisions for himself. Cheetahs don't like to eat what they didn't use their speed and strength to kill.

Indeed, it is perfectly fine for a woman to help her man accomplish goals, and to assist in areas in the event of emergencies. But if you have been with a man that is comfortable with you doing everything for him in the field of providing basic needs, you're definitely not dealing with a cheetah.

The cheetah has a unique cosmetic feature strategically designed on its face. There is a tear-like stripe that flows from the eyes and connects to its mouth, symbolizing that VISION must flow to the tongue. When dealing with a mature man spiritually, he will have the ability to connect what he sees through what he says. As women, you don't have the ability to see what a man sees, so he must be able to clearly articulate his vision through his conversations with you.

Continually negative people are a direct result of the lack of keen vision, and these are usually people that are not able to see past present circumstances into a brighter future. Women do not handle pressure in the same manner as men. So, if the woman, as the weaker vessel, can't draw strength from a man who can communicate to them that even in tough situations that everything will be alright, the woman may panic out of a man's failure to emotionally secure her.

Women have a tough time submitting to a vision that is not clear, so a man must be able to cast vision in the relationship, and a wise woman will help facilitate the path towards getting there. Men must be encouraged to use their full potential, and be fueled with the motivation, that just like the cheetah, they are at the top of the ladder in what they do.

If you're single and have a tough time honoring or respecting men, you can throw away your dreams of having a healthy relationship with one. How you handle your relationships while out in public socializing, usually determines the level of peace you have behind closed doors. If you embarrass the person you're with, in public, it will not end well for you in private. Another known fact about cheetahs is they usually like to eat in private so that other animals don't see it and start confrontation as it is a known fact that cheetahs do not like to fight as it relates to confrontation.

You may wonder why men go into a mode of shutting down during confrontations. Contrary to popular belief, men don't mind communicating. We just don't like the confrontation or the loud theatrics of getting in his face, finger-pointing, name-calling, hollering, yelling, and screaming. It is usually at those moments that the pride a man has of his gender rises within him, causing the whole atmosphere to go south. King Solomon, a man who asked God for wisdom, said in Proverbs 15: 1 "A gentle answer turns away wrath, but a harsh word stirs up anger."

Conflict resolution is as simple as having a mature adult conversation about things. I have learned in life that there is not much a conversation cannot fix when it relates to issues of any kind. Though men attempt to internalize, we are terrible at hiding things, and our attempt to conceal things is always detected by a woman.

An interesting fact about cheetahs is they are the only cat that cannot fully retract their claws, only a partial semi retracts. The genus name -Acinonyx- means "no-move-claw" in Greek. Men are terrible at hiding things from a woman, and in the end, it's pointless to even try and do so. Just as the cheetah, we attempt to retract truths, retract feelings, and re-tract uncertainties, only to have them still revealed.

It is a fail-proof system put in place by God that will always give you the intuition to know when something is wrong with the man in your life. Use the gift not to make him feel vulnerable but to be strategic in your approach to encourage him towards feeling safe enough to share his heart when things are troubling him.

Nothing makes a person feel more secure emotionally than the freedom that exposure brings. Yes, exposure is actually freedom; this is what being naked and not ashamed is about, to have someone know all of your faults, fears, and failures. The pressure to cover up areas and hide things for the sake of living up to a certain image is a full-time job for most people. What people actually fear is being exploited by people waiting to benefit in a selfish manner from using your truths to their advantage. This is what a person expects from outsiders and therefore puts up walls and safety measures to prevent people from getting to close. However, it is a burden too great to bear when you do not feel safe enough to be emotionally naked in front of your close loved ones.

In relationships, we should create atmospheres that are conducive to being transparent to that no one at any time is a prisoner to voicing their feelings. Women, if you can master this craft, there is no conversation the man in your life will ever avoid. If you are dealing with someone who is just a complete liar, then this is a separate issue altogether.

One of the most exhausting things you can do is argue with a liar and prove to them that they are lying. These individuals have created a reality for themselves that doesn't abide by facts. The most ironic thing about this type of person is that you know they are not truthful, and they know that you know they are not truthful. The best remedy for dealing with this type of individual is to shrug your shoulders and not waste your valuable time. Don't you for one single second let it disturb your peace. Keep it moving.

In my conclusion, a cheetah does not walk in situations that it is gifted to run. Therefore, like the cheetah, a man must possess drive and determination to pursue his destiny with the utmost sense of urgency. Do not restrict or hinder a purpose-driven man. Instead, invest in his dreams by providing the love, support, and nurturing necessary to see his vision bloom.

Chapter Eight

Let
HER
Leopard

So, if men are Cheetahs, women are Leopards! The first thing to understand about this feline called a leopard is that its spot is different. Most leopards have dark spots on their fur. These spots are called "rosettes" because their shape is similar to that of a rose flower. Therefore, the leopard's hide is uniquely set apart from the spot design of the cheetah. It does not spend time trying to look like a cheetah, because its design is so unique. That being said, once a woman embraces the things that brand her distinctively from the man, it's an empowerment to maximize them. A woman that is truly comfortable and confident in the skin she's in is never intimidated by the role a man plays because she knows she has her own spot and purpose in life.

The question is often asked, "Where would the world be without women?" As the crown of creation, I can tell you that nothing would have been birthed without the woman. No matter how fast the cheetah is or it's natural-born abilities, there are things that the cheetah doesn't have the strength to do. Leopards are silent creatures, not announcing themselves in the atmospheres, but only occasionally emitting a cough-like call.

A leopard's prey never hears them coming. They go

in silently, get the job done, and let the trophy of the kill speak the loudest. Leopards find no glory in using roars to prove its presence, unlike others in the cat family. In turn, a wise woman that knows her strengths finds no pleasure in screaming matches with her male counterpart because she can use subtlety to bring the exact results she wants.

Noise is not always a sign of power, and quietness is not always a sign of weakness. Leopards are skilled climbers, making them unique with how they consume their prey after a kill. Often, they drag their heavy prey up into trees to feast out on limbs as they feel right at home eating in high places. Men, if you are reading this section and wonder why the lady of your life loves to dine in high-priced restaurants, it's because it's in her nature to be in high places. This does not mean a leopard can't adjust and eat in any atmosphere, but the genetic makeup of the leopard seems to find delight in elevated environments.

What's fascinating about them is no matter how high they climb, they always know how to find their way back down to ground level, which speaks to the humility a woman should have no matter how high her accomplishments and achievements are in life. It can be a huge turnoff to men when a woman is flamboyant. There are many cases in life where women are at the top of the corporate ladder as owners, CEO's, managers. This type of diversity in our times is to be celebrated, as women are well capable of handling any of these roles. However, not at the expense of replacing the role of a man, but rather working in conjunction as our counterparts.

Leopards prefer solitude over socializing and spend most of their time alone. They each have their specific territory and leave scratches on trees, and urine scent marks to warn other leopards to <u>stay</u> away! It's common amongst most women to share a similar story of not having many female friends in life and to be comfortable in solitude. This usually is a learned behavior, due to the lack of being able to trust individuals in their space, who don't continue to fail them.

Women are very territorial over what's theirs, and it's a fair warning, do not mess with what they have marked as being their own. Although a leopard is generally a quiet species, they do growl when they're angry. Women, no matter how sweet and innocent they may seem, each possesses another side of them that can become your worst nightmare when triggered.

The Investment of Love

The claws of leopards are retractable, meaning they can conceal things that can hurt you. Women also have this ability to conceal things that can hurt a man. Men are not mind readers, but a man must be willing to communicate and hear the heart of the lady in his life. Daily Questions as simple as, "How was your day?" become the door opener to many potential conversations.

It's critical to realize that people may look ok on the outside, but you never know what's truly on a person's mind. There is not much a woman won't tell you if she's asked. She may not initially volunteer it, but if asked directly, she will not avoid it. With this being said, a woman wants to genuinely feel a man is interested in what's on her mind, and that her voice matters. She wants to be heard. A woman is always sharing her heart, but the question is, "With who?"

Women must have an outlet to express themselves to someone genuinely interested in what they have to say. Sometimes that go-to individual for a woman is her mom, her sister, or possibly even another man who has shown interest in a willingness to listen. Women are naturally loyal, and being creatures of habit helps their loyalty. If she is willing to take the risk of going outside of her relationship, it's only because there is an area she is not being nurtured in, and nothing entices a woman quicker than what she hears. This point is proven by the serpent's ability to deceive Eve in the Garden of Eden. Adam was not present during the serpent's conversation, which speaks to the principle a man must be a continued presence in the life of the lady he is with, not only physically, but this is the result of a man who is not present emotionally.

The woman lives for the interactions of communicating. It is their number one form of intimacy, and whoever meets the demand of that need has the most influence on them.

Another major strength of Leopards is they are capable of carrying animals heavier than themselves. The one thing most women are faced with doing in life is carrying something or someone else's load that's heavier than them. In fact, many wish to share this burden with someone, but the reality is that most men are afraid of the challenge of helping her carry the weight. This causes her to step up in areas, not out of desire, but out of necessity. The problem with stepping up out of necessity is it often causes them not to know how to turn that side off when someone comes into their life to assist in the areas others fell short. They deal with it because women are creatures of habit and quickly learn to adapt to situations.

If one is to have them lower their guard, it can take a consistent track record of seeing proven results, to overcome their tendency of total independence. Finally, the question was once asked, would a leopard attack a human? An injured **leopard** may become an exclusive predator of livestock if it is unable to kill their normal prey since domesticated animals typically lack natural defenses. Frequent livestock-raiding may cause **leopards** to lose their fear of **humans**, and shooting injuries may have caused some **leopards** to become man-eaters.

Dangerous things happen when a leopard is pushed beyond its limits, and so it is with a woman who has been pushed beyond her limits as well. Being severely injured can take a leopard's character or woman out of her normal character. When this happens, things that are usually safe have now become a target. The old statement says it this way, "Hell has no fury like a woman scorned."

The return a woman gives is often a direct response to the seed she is given. Give her a house. She gives you a home. Give her seed. She gives you a child. Give her affection. She gives you romance. Alternatively, a different man can bring out different results from the same woman. As earlier mentioned, because of a woman's nature of adapting to her environment, she will try to emulate her man's lifestyle in the public eye. If he is a corporate professional, out of natural reaction, she will be more corporate. If he is religious, she will be more modest in her appearance.

The energy a woman receives is the energy she will release. A wise man will use this ability to his advantage and understand he has the power to determine what type of woman she is based on how he handles her.

In my close of this thought, when leopards are born, they are completely blind, thus dependent on their mothers for care. Symbolically, a woman is born without vision. She must receive the proper nurturing and care she needs in the infant and childhood stages of her development. The presence of the mother in her daughter's life is equally important as the presence of a father in his son's life. If a young girl is to gain her clarity, over time, she must be presented with an untainted and clear view.

The first seeds of relationships a daughter receives

are not when she is of age to enter one. The first seeds are when she is first able to observe the relationships her mother has with others. Mothers, you have a responsibility that no matter what things were like in your relationships, not to damage your daughter's desire or ideal of pursuing healthy relationships in her life.

Whether married, single, or dating, your children deserve to be aimed in the right direction. This has to be intentional and on purpose, that you refuse to talk negatively about what love is, after all; God is Love. The book of 1 John 4:18 says, "There is no fear in love; but perfect love casteth out fear: because fear hath torment. He that feareth is not made perfect in love."

Don't be guilty of making others afraid or fear love because of your personal past experiences in life. The burden of, "What if it doesn't work out," is the torment a woman has when gripped by the hands of fear. A woman must not allow the start to stop her. The biggest issue in pursuing healthy relationships is the willingness to be open to starting them. The day of being so emotionally afraid to trust and love again is over. So what? You may have had some bad experiences in life, but that is no reason not to be hopeful over where God is taking you. Even the bad experiences in life are lessons learned; if not about others, then these experiences taught us more about us.

God has created the woman strong and beautiful. Just as we see the beauty of leopards, celebrating their strengths, we must commend the women as the crown of creation for the feline family! Let the woman in your life be strong, let her be free, and let her be beautiful; Let her Leopard!

Chapter Nine

When Fathers Release Sons

CHAPTER NINE—When Fathers Release Sons

A story that seems to be common among most Millennials is the truth of growing up in fatherless homes. Television shows are filled with emotional stories of individuals trying to reconnect with their fathers desperately, or either the regret of not having them present in their daily lives. It is no secret the impact it makes in a child to have a healthy relationship with their father. The biggest reason for fatherless homes is because of divorce. In recent years, there has been a trend of positive change with millennials that is beginning to change as it relates to the divorce rate. Young people in the United States are rebelling against their parents' generation, though not in a way that you might expect.

According to statista.com, the US divorce rate began falling in the early 1990s and has since continued on an overall downward trend. In 1992, there were 4.8 divorces per 1,000 population. By 2016, this had dropped to 3.2. The falling divorce rate may have a lot to do with millennials' attitudes toward marriage. Analysis of <u>American Community Survey (ACS) data by Philip Cohen</u>, a sociology professor at the University of Maryland, suggests young people are doing things differently to previous generations. Unlike baby boomers who married young regardless of their circumstances, millennials – and some Gen Xers – are choosing to marry once they have completed their education, have established their careers, and have sound finances. New research suggests Americans in their late 20s have a less than 50% chance of getting divorced (Wood, 2015).

Meanwhile, their chances of staying married are increasing. As many things as millennials are blamed for being the source of the problem, what if we are the generation to turn things around in the areas the generations before failed. The question to take from this, however, is, "How is it that the generation coming from the highest level of fatherless and divorchomes, increasing the number of successful married families?" How are they this effective not having seen good examples? How can they be a good father when they didn't have a present father? I'm glad you asked.

A story comes to mind from Genesis regarding a child who did not have a father present in his life by the name of Ishmael. The name Ishmael in Hebrew means "God Will Hear." This name was given directly to Hagar by God as he heard her misery from her mistress Sarai being mad at her for a situation, she put her in. It was the idea of Sarai to give Hagar to her husband since she could not have children at the time. Hagar, at the request of her master, became the side chick and was punished for a situation she didn't put herself in by herself.

Let us look to The New International Version of the bible regarding this story, Genesis 16:6- 9 states:

6 "Your slave is in your hands," Abram said. "Do with her whatever you think best." Then Sarai mistreated Hagar; so she fled from her.

7 The angel of the Lord found Hagar near a spring in the desert; it was the spring that is beside the <u>road</u> to Shur. **8** And he said, "Hagar, slave of Sarai, where have you come from, and where are you going?"

"I'm running away from my mistress Sarai," she answered.

9 Then the angel of the Lord told her, "Go back to your mistress and submit to her." **10** The angel added, "I will increase your descendants so much that they will be too numerous to count."

11 The angel of the Lord also said to her: "You are now pregnant and you will give birth to a son. You shall name him Ishmael,[a]for the Lord has heard of your misery.

12 He will be a wild donkey of a man; his hand will be against everyone and everyone's hand against him, and he will <u>live</u> in hostility toward[b] all his brothers."

Notice, God doesn't ever recommend running away from situations but encourages us to face them head-on, as he did with Hagar by telling her to go back and deal with the situation. Her comfort to go back into a hostile environment was the consolation of knowing God heard the cry of a mother who was placed in circumstances beyond her control and gave a promise that her son would be blessed. Her concern, as with any mother, was the well-being of her son moving forward should things not work out with Abram. As we look closer at the following scriptures, not only is he the God who hears us, but he is also the God who sees us.

13 She gave this name to the Lord who spoke to her: "You are the God who sees me," for she said, "I have now seen[c] the One who sees me." **14** That is why the well was called Beer Lahai Roi[d]; it is still there, between Kadesh and Bered.

We know the character of God by how he acts towards us. Hagar called God El-Roi, which means "the God who sees me." Although Hagar ran away to a place that no tangible person was able to see, the angel of the Lord found her. Sometimes we are in a room full of individuals yet feel invisible to the world, in relationships, and, however, feel alone. But even when people don't know where we are, and we wonder does anyone even see me in my emotional anguish, our father is El-Roi; He sees us!

15 So Hagar bore Abram, a son, and Abram gave the name Ishmael to the son she had borne. **16** Abram was eighty -six years old when Hagar bore him Ishmael.

Genesis 21: 9 -15

9 But Sarah saw that the son whom Hagar the Egyptian had borne to Abraham was mocking, **10** and she said to Abraham, "Get rid of that slave woman and her son, for that woman's son will never share in the inheritance with my son Isaac."

11 The matter distressed Abraham greatly because it concerned his son.**12** But God said to him, "Do not be so distressed about the boy and your slave woman. Listen to whatever Sarah tells you, because it is through Isaac that your offspring[b] will be reckoned. **13** I will make the son of the slave into a nation also, because he is your offspring."

14 Early the next morning Abraham took some food and a skin of <u>water</u> and gave them to Hagar. He set them on

The Investment of Love

her shoulders and then sent her off with the boy. She went on her way and wandered in the Desert of Beersheba.

15 When the water in the skin was gone, she put the boy under one of the bushes. **16** Then she went off and sat down about a bowshot away, for she thought, "I cannot watch the boy die." And as she sat there, she[c] began to sob.

17 God heard the boy crying, and the angel of God called to Hagar from heaven and said to her, "What is the matter, Hagar? Do not be afraid; God has heard the boy crying as he lies there. **18** Lift the boy up and take him by the hand, for I will make him into a great nation."

19 Then God opened her eyes, and she saw a well of water. So she went and filled the skin with water and gave the boy a drink.

20 God was with the boy as he grew up. He lived in the desert and became an archer. **21** While he was living in the Desert of Paran, his mother got a wife for him from Egypt.

For 13 years, Hagar and Ishmael lived under the same roof as Abram and Sarai. Until God changed their names to Abraham and Sarah; this was the timing he was to fulfill the prophecy of giving them their son together by the name of

Isaac. Sarah could no longer stand to see Ishmael as it was a mockery to her to be reminded of the decision she made to give Hagar to Abraham. She told Abraham to force them to leave the house. Even God told Abraham, "Whatever your wife Sarah suggests, listen to her." Abraham, without question, told Hagar and Ishmael it was time to leave sending them off with only a bit of food and a skin of water.

Abraham was known to be a wealthy man in those times, yet because of the request of his wife, he released his son Ishmael and his mistress Hagar, without any inheritance or money of any sort. This may have seemed harsh to some that God would recommend Abraham in listening to his wife Sarah to put them out. However, when Man releases you, it still does not change the promise God has on your life. The angel of the Lord had already given Hagar a promise 13 years before this event, that he heard and saw her and would make Ishmael a great nation. So, this eviction to them was the move that would put the process of the promise in motion.

It's important to know that the promises of God are a process. We often rejoice when the promise is made, but don't consider the chain of events that have to happen while

The Investment of Love

we are on our way to obtaining what God declared we would have. This story is so relevant for what so many children with absent father's face. A mother who was a third party in a relationship as a result of an affair is often put away, and a father is absent from the life of their child birthed from it, at the request of keeping his marriage happy. The mother is left solely to invest the love and provision into a child she did not produce on her own.

Children who are raised in this fashion often learn of their half-siblings later who live in the home with their father in common being provided for in luxury, while you suffer as an outsider with barely enough to make ends meet at times. However, their departure would be a blessing in disguise for both Ishmael and his mother. While she was wondering on her way with her son to the desert of Beersheba, they ran out of both food and water. It was at this moment that human nature kicked in. She took Ishmael down and walked away from him to vent and cry.

As parents, sometimes, we don't wish for our children to see us at vulnerable moments. Many times, we face problems our children have no idea of because we use discretion, so they won't panic that we don't have things under control.

Hagar, not knowing where their provisions or next meal would come from, had given up all hope as she could not stand to see Ishmael starve to death. While Hagar was away crying, Ishmael begins to cry as well. I'm sure hunger pains begin to kick in. This was a feeling he had never known while he was in Abraham's house; everything was always plenteous. The thought probably crossed his mind as to why his father could put him out just like that, without caring enough to keep him and his mother both. The child in these situations is always innocent as they had no control over their being born.

Sitting with mixed emotions and countenance full of anguish, Ishmael begins to cry out. It was at that very moment, the angel of the Lord speaks to Hagar and says, "Fear not! I have heard the boys cry." He then opens her eyes and reveals to her she was near the life source of water the whole time. Even in the toughest of times of man's extremity, we are closer to what shall sustain us than we think. Hagar filled the skin with water and gave drink to her son Ishmael.

From that point, everything in Ishmael's life shifted as the scripture tells us. God was with the boy as he grew up. When fathers release their sons, sons can yet make it because

The Investment of Love

although a father may not be with them, The Father is. If God is for you, he is more than the whole world against you. Ishmael went on to become a great archer/hunter without having received one lesson from his natural father on how to hunt.

Earlier, I stated that sometimes people wonder why millennials are so successful in areas where there was no one to teach them. It's because God extends a level of grace to individuals just as Ishmael had to do things no man has ever taken the time to teach you.

Many success stories are told of top-achieving athletes breaking records, and never had a present father to play catch with them or record their times while running. However, when God is with you, you must understand you have your own promise that is not predicated by who stays or walks out of your life. When fathers release sons, it becomes the moment that they must use their own voice so that God will hear your cry. David wrote in Psalms 116:1, "I love the LORD because he hath heard my voice *and* my supplications." Our God hears, he sees, and is gracing this millennial generation with the desire to turn things around and become the fathers and husbands for their families they have always dreamed.

Chapter Ten

Dating with a Purpose

The subject of dating for someone entering the mingling stage can present itself with an overwhelming challenge. Countless mental hours and effort can go into knowing who is right and who is wrong for your life. Dating is a necessary process that cannot be skipped by anyone who desires a lasting and healthy relationship.

There is no such thing as love at first sight. There is only attraction at first sight. It may be the way someone physically appeals to you that initially gains your interest, but true love can only come from a bond formed over time. Many people don't only understand how to date effectively, but neither how to effectively communicate. If you're seeking a healthy relationship, the two must go hand and hand to accomplish!

Dating during any phase of your relationship is important; whether you're dating before marriage or married, you still need to date. Some man asked, "How do we define what counts as a date?" What are the qualifiers of an evening for it to count as a date? Is it just going out to the movies or dinner? The whole purpose of dating in the beginning stages is to get to know someone. Getting to know someone cannot be accomplished without spending time with, because anything that you love you will spend time with to prove your love.

Couples that have been together for a while often make the mistake of not continuing to date continually. They usually end up slacking off as it relates to the time they spend with one another. The newness of anything will lose its luster if we do not intentionally keep things fresh, and scheduling regular dates with one another can help to achieve this.

We often get lost in the hustle and bustle of life through careers, kids, and other responsibilities. We must view our relationships just as much of a responsibility as anything else in our lives and make an effort to date on purpose. Many people are guilty of investing years of their time, and still, do not know each other.

When you date, you want to spend time communicating with one another, going to the movies, or any other activity that one or both of you may enjoy. While you may be around one another physically, it is time spent hearing and being entertained by someone else. So, the danger in doing this is there's still no personal intimacy time of allowing each other to learn more about the other.

The science behind knowing when to marry someone is not determined by a set timeline, but rather a point in the relationship to where you know them. Some have dated and gotten married as early as six (6) months from meeting each other. From personal experience, my wife and I dated for three (3) years before tying the knot. It took us three (3) years to thoroughly know each other well enough to get married. I am thankful we didn't succumb to the opinions and pressure of others wanting us to do it quickly.

During those three (3) years, we experienced two (2) breakups and an engagement that was once called off. Each of these was great for us to experience before tying the knot because, after three (3) chances of trying to call it quits, we were consistently led back to one another. I'm amazed at the number of individuals who are willing to enter something long term and haven't ever experienced a good argument with one another. Lots of truths are exposed when an individual is upset with you. When conflicts are presented within a relationship, it's the perfect opportunity to see how each other behaves under pressure. If there are never any disputes or arguments in a relationship, rest assured someone is being taken advantage of or someone is faking.

The Investment of Love

There was a television game show titled The Newly Weds, which launched in 1966 that ran successfully for many years and had its final episode to air in 2013. *The Newlywed Game* show pits newly married couples against each other in a series of revealing rounds of questions about how well the spouses knew or did not know each other.

Regularly, you were able to see a couple who failed at how answering questions correctly, proving that they didn't know their spouse too well. The answers were often a prime example of being around someone for a length of time, realizing that you don't actually know them. When we do not know the individuals with whom we are getting involved, it is a huge mistake to get married.

I want to paint a picture for you and tell you of a true story that People magazine covered once on a lady named Su Yun in the Yunnan province of China. While she and her family were on vacation, she bought what she believed to be a Tibetan Mastiff puppy and took it back home. Once she got the animal home, each of the family members was surprised at its huge appetite. They thought that for it to be a dog, they told reporters they didn't understand why it would chow down on a box of fruit and two buckets of noodles every day.

This went on for some time until the pet reached 250 pounds and started walking around on its hind legs.

At that point, the family realized the dog they thought they took home was a mistake. What they thought to be a dog was an Asiatic Black Bear. Su Yun, although having cared for the bear and built a relationship with it, in fear of what the bear could do to her family, called the proper wildlife authorities to remove it.

This story turns out to not end tragically for the bear nor the family that cared for it. There are, however, so many scenarios that could have gone wrong with this entire picture. However, it teaches a valuable lesson on so many levels. Su Yun wanted a pet so badly that she was willing to take something home without first inspecting what it was.

In the infant stages, the bear resembled the species of the Tibetan Mastiff dog. Because it looked like a dog on its outside appearance, without any further investigation, Su Yun made a huge mistake and brought home a bear. Don't be like her and bring home a bear because you desire to have a dog so badly.

Many men and women make this same mistake each day by wanting a man or a woman so badly that we will go solely on the outward appearance of an individual. Just because someone looks like what we think we want, it's wise to invest the time in actually checking to see if the person is who they appear to be.

Time reveals all, and as time passes, it tells the true nature of an individual. It wasn't until the bear stood up on its hind legs that thought came to Su Yun that she didn't have a dog but rather a bear. If you don't get into a rush, you will see for yourself whether or not the man or woman is what and who they say they are on paper.

Every man and woman does many similar basic things that won't let you depict the type of person you're dealing with initially. We all laugh, talk, sleep, and breathe, which are not the signs that determine our true character. Just as the bear was not initially recognizable by its massive appetite because all dogs eat, we have our similar traits as well. Su Yun knew immediately, however, that dogs don't stand up in this fashion, and that was her sign that she was dealing with a beast that could quickly destroy her and her family.

Single men and women raising families must be careful when bringing someone else into your household and moving in a person who, over time, can end up being dangerous to the well-being of you and your family. For Su Yun, the story ended without anyone being hurt, but that's because she was wise enough to release it and not let the need for the bond blind her from making a wise decision. The fact that she spent two years building a relationship, she still made the conscious choice to take the loss on time invested in protecting her loved ones, as opposed to keeping the bear.

There is a popular and true quote from the famous poet Maya Angelou, who wrote, "When someone shows you who they are, believe them the first time." People know themselves much better than you do. That's why it's important to stop expecting them to be something other than who they are."

So many people in life continue to ignore the signs they are given about individuals until one day it is too late, and they are put in a fatal situation.

After much history with someone, it's tough to think of starting over. However, the loss of time is better than a life of torment, torture, and possibly loss of life. No relationship in life is worth sacrificing your peaceful mentality, your sanity, or your physical well-being. In all investments, it is better to cut your losses early versus getting to the point of no return and end up losing everything.

There is a common denominator to every failed relationship you have had in life, and that common factor is you. You have to not only know the other person, but you also have to know YOU! If you get into with everyone you connect with, everyone else is not the problem. You are the problem. We have to figure out what it is about ourselves that continually cause us to clash with others.

Be willing to invest the time necessary into yourself to become emotionally whole again before getting involved in something prematurely. If you do not have the emotional resources and reserves to invest in someone else, marriage is not for you. In the world of math, two halves make a whole, but as it relates to relationships to people that are not whole will not establish a relationship that's whole. Individuals who are broken, but are hopeless romantics, will even attempt to string you along their journey of trying to find peace while detaining you of yours.

Never exclusively invest or commit your NOW to someone who can't tell you what's NEXT! Beware of the people who forever use manipulation, selling dreams of "One day..." commitments that never manifest.

There was a cartoon where a horse rider would mount a horse with a fishing pole with a dangling carrot in the face of the horse. This tactic was used to continually get the horse to walk in its desired direction without ever being able to obtain the prize, the carrot. You need people in your life that will continue to pursue you, even though you are already theirs. Someone who can consistently show you the beauty of yourself that you look past while viewing yourself in the mirror each day. Life is not about just having moments but creating memories with someone. Whether you are single, in a relationship, or married, every date you make is an opportunity to draw closer to one another.

Never waste a planned date discussing problems or using that special time together to sort out issues as those are things that can be dealt with at another time. There's a time and a place for all things, and the time set aside to enjoy one another is not the proper time. Do not discuss or entertain anything that is not conducive to the enjoyment of the time you have set aside for that purpose. Control your environment while you are together. By controlling yourself, you can prevent distractions like answering calls and text messages, no matter who they are from. Train your children that your alone time with the one you're dating (especially spouse) is important, and should not be interrupted unless it is an extreme emergency.

Don't leave a subject this important to chance, or think that it will happen whenever it happens. We must intentionally make it happen, and date with a purpose!

Chapter Eleven

Communicating On Purpose

If there is one thing overall that any relationship must have, it is COMMUNICATION! In this generation, it often said that Marriage is obsolete. Marriage, however, is the first type of relationship that was created and ordained by God. To say that God created an institution that would have an expiration date for relevance is an error in one's thinking.

The decrease in morale to enter into this sacred covenant has been influenced by the constant rise of divorce, infidelity, and private problems posted publicly on social media. Public platforms have a way of magnifying the negatives, as bad news travels faster than celebrating the positive, it can leave couples and singles hopeless. But there is yet hope! Fortunately, all of the previously mentioned issues that are deterring individuals from jumping the broom are a direct result of the lack of communication.

All marriages/relationships have the potential to fail or succeed. Depending on the level of commitment and faithfulness, two individuals are willing to invest. Commitment and faithfulness are two different things, and it takes both in play for a relationship to work. Commitment is a pledge or promise, but faithfulness is the follow-through of what you committed to doing. Don't make the mistake of being committed to something that you are not faithful in following through to completion. The most attractive quality a man or woman can display is to do exactly what they say they will do. When a person is consistent in their follow-through, it is the glue that will seal trust in a relationship.

Open communication has to be the foundation of any relationship. Communication face to face or audibly works best, as communication through text or message can be taken out of context because it has no audible tone to express the sincerity in which it was intended. Digital hearts and cyber kisses can't replace the impact of verbally telling someone you love them or the feeling of physical affection. Part of effective communication is being a great listener, and everyone wants and deserves the right to be heard. The key to listening is no matter what a person says, if you are forming an opinion while someone else is explaining, you are not actually listening, you are judging or trying to figure out a response. If you often interrupt others in mid-conversation, it proves your pre-judging and not listening.

I've discovered in life that there is not much that a conversation can't fix. If you come into a discussion with your guard up, then you came prepared for a fight. You are in a relationship, not a boxing ring, but when people do not know how to effectively communicate, out of ignorance, they attack each other. On average, it is said that women speak about 20,000 words per day, and men only speak about 7,000 per day. So, women are talking too much, and men are not talking enough.

There has to be balanced communication in your relationships for them to remain healthy. So, if you are in a relationship/marriage asking, "When will things change," my answer is, "When you are ready to talk about it." The world is continuously changing the way we communicate; the invention of the rotary telephone was a breakthrough in technology. People took great pride and joy in closing the gap of long-distance by being able to give someone a phone call. However, as technology progressed, the internet was introduced, and the start of creating free email accounts was beginning to take the lead; business owners, employers, and Corporate America almost mandated the importance of switching to this form of communication out of convenience.

Somewhere in the thick of it all, cell phones became more popular and accessible to consumers and integrated its unique form of communication called texting. Seeing the popularity of this form of staying connected, Social Media then took the world by storm and created its form of messenger communications. Now our most popular form of communications and expressions are no longer in an audible format. Typing a post, sending a text, and creating an email doesn't even require an individual to use their voice.

As I stated earlier, a key component of effective communication is a great listener, and everyone wants and deserves the right to be heard. When the energy of a person's voice is no longer there for listening, we have taken a key ingredient out of communications whole intent to connect intimately. The biggest downfall to texting is people lose meaning in 'words only' style of communication. So, you have to strive to be as clear as possible when texting because it can cause what was meant to be said with good intentions to be taken out of context because there is no audible expression.

The danger with the social media age is when someone doesn't have social media etiquette, the platform it gives can be very harmful to a relationship. People will live in the same house, but instead of communicating about a private issue, they will air it out publicly on Facebook or other platforms. Employees will work in the same company one office down from their coworkers but will take to social media to settle a dispute. People who talk in private to settle a matter want a solution, but people who complain in public about another want public attention.

Be careful not to entertain the bait of an individual who comes for you openly through a public platform. Their intentions are not pure, and it's not worth the investment of time. A fool needs no assistance in making themselves look like one, and anyone with any intelligence will always settle matters one on one in private.

A stable relationship cannot be built on flirtatious remarks, as flirting is not a serious form of relationship purposed communication. If someone comes into your life and the only subject matter of their conversation is what they desire to do to you physically, they lack the depth of having an actual conversation. It reveals that their only intentions are what lead to a sexual agenda. With people like this, if you do not play into their motive, they will soon phase themselves out of your life. Let them move on to what will feed into their scheme. People like this who leave are not a loss. They make room for someone to enter your life that can reach your mind on an intellectual, spiritual, and emotional level.

As you age in life, you begin to desire companionship over company. Company is a number of individuals assembled, while companionship is the feeling of fellowship and friendship. This is the reason younger people enjoy a crowd, but older people prefer to enjoy the camaraderie of select individuals who feed the desire for true fellowship and friendship. It doesn't take a lot of people to have a good time together. If you rely on a crowd around you to enjoy the person you're in a relationship with, then there is no genuine connection with one another.

We must have realistic expectations and deny the myth of thinking that perfect relationships exist. With humanity being imperfect, how can we expect two flawed individuals to enter into something, without mistakes or faults? The goal is not perfection; it's completion. What you lack in life the other individual should possess and compensate. Yin and Yang, through night and day, is the balance that it takes to create true harmony.

My best advice for anyone wanting a successful relationship is to Love Always, Communicate Frequently, Forgive Quickly, and Laugh Often! Be open and transparent in your communication with your loved ones, as people can't cover what they are unaware of needs to be covered. You cannot hold someone accountable for the mishandling of an issue of which you never made them aware.

I have always found the work of a defense attorney interesting, as it is their job to represent both the guilty and the innocent. The most important factor for them to be able to do their job effectively is to know the truth; it's not their job to judge you on your truth but only to protect you in your defense. They always ask a client, "Are you guilty, or did you do what your being accused of?" This doesn't change their ability to defend you. It just better prepares them for how they need to do their job to help you in your situation effectively. Once on the defense stand, if the prosecutors expose things that they were unaware of, it renders them powerless to protect you.

Telling the truth upfront about things is the mature thing to do as it allows an individual the choice as to what they are willing to represent. Some truths are deal-breakers, but that's better than hiding the truth, causing someone to learn later what they would have chosen not to invest their time into initially. Most Lawyers like to know the full truth upfront so that they can choose whether to accept the case or not. Although some lawyers won't take your case and represent you, rest assured others will. It may be a greater expense, but someone is comfortable and confident in moving forward with you regardless of what you have done.

People in life regarding relationships are the same way when you are honest with a person in communicating your truth. Some may check out by not choosing to move forward with you, and that's perfectly fine. There will always be someone who can handle your pains and your past. That's what amazing grace does; it looks beyond our faults and sees our needs.

Remember, when communicating, timing is everything.

Although certain things need to be stated, that should not wait. Other things should not happen upon the first contact with someone in whom you find interest. Can you imagine the response you would get if someone asked your name, and your reply was, "Hi, I'm broken!" Though it may be true, it's the wrong timing, and you will never have a second chance to make a good first impression.

Even in Marriage, timing on when you communicate things is critical. The type of response and understanding you will get towards particular subject matters, no matter how important they may be, often depend on the time presented. Women, if your husband comes in from a hard day at work, your first initial greeting should not be about a problem of any kind, or a financial responsibility of any kind. It may be the right conversation to have, but if it's not done at the correct time, the response you get from him may escalate an even greater issue between the two of you.

The first question to ask when greeting your spouse after work is, "How was your day?" Asking this accomplishes two things: First, it shows your spouse your concern about their well-being. Second, this will allow them to express any concerns or cares they have had throughout the day. Based on how they answer, this question will show you what type of mood and vibe they have had for the day and will give you a strategy of how to entreat them going forward. Give them some time and allow them to get their mind off of the previous portion of their day, and even assist them in doing so with tender loving care. Use your discernment as to whether something can wait for another day altogether or if the timing is right. Once they return to good spirits, express it.

Even in your expression, it's not about what you say. It's how you say it. Never speak something in an aggressive tone, no matter what it's regarding. The energy you give out is what will boomerang back to you. So, express things in the tone in which you expect to receive. Communication, if done frequently, is the lifeline towards any relationship in our life. Silence is generally the sign the life of something is fading. Silence can also be interpreted in so many ways by someone your silent towards, so be willing to communicate. If you do not want your friends, family, or spouse to assume the worse, then never make the mistake of not talking when need be. Make an effort at all times to communicate on purpose!

Chapter Twelve

Public Front, Private Fun

CHAPTER TWELVE—Public Front, Private Fun

The first relationship we see in the bible is the relationship between Adam & Eve. Imagine what their bond was like for Adam to be persuaded into disobeying a direct order from God, the father. He was clearly told not to eat from the tree of knowledge of good and evil, for the day you do that you will surely die. Eve then makes the mistake that many individuals have made who came after her. She allowed an outside source to influence an internal commitment she had with her husband.

Both Adam and Eve had committed to one another and to obey the commandment of God; abstain from eating of the tree of the knowledge of good and evil. The Serpent caught Eve the moment she was alone and away from the covering of her husband. He began to try and influence her that it was, in fact, ok to eat of the Tree of Good & Evil. In response, she told him exactly what God had commanded them, "If we do eat of it, we will die."

The Serpent immediately responded (Genesis 3:4-5), "And the serpent said unto the woman, you shall not surely die: For God know that in the day ye eat thereof, then your eyes shall be opened, and ye shall be as gods, knowing good and evil." Something to key in on is the fact that once Eve looked on the fruit and it was pleasant to the eyes. She knew it would make her wise, so she ate of the fruit. At that point, her eyes were opened, and she now saw Adam differently. At this very moment, Adam had yet to partake in eating the fruit.

Genesis 3:7 lets us know that after they both ate of the fruit, they both realized they were physically naked, and out of embarrassment, they sewed fig leaves together and made a covering of aprons to hide their bodies.

Imagine with me for a moment that the moment Eve ate, and she saw Adam differently her reaction to what she being described to her husband Adam how he looked. Before Adam ate the fruit himself, he could only go by what eve was explaining to him how she saw things.

Up to this point, they had always seen and viewed each other the same way. Their nakedness was a truth the whole time, but they had never seen one another as naked, and therefore, they could live perfectly exposed to one another and not be worried about the public's view. Adam's curiosity in what she described pushed him to the point of disobedience because he couldn't imagine living life, not being able to see each other the same.

The breakdown in all of this is that the Serpent (the

public) had been watching them the whole time and because he never saw them eating from the tree of the knowledge of good and evil, but yet eating and enjoying every other tree in the garden he used crafty and cunning words to approach them. In so many words, he said, "I see you out doing this and doing that, but I never see you enjoying eating from this tree of knowledge of good and evil. God must have told you that you couldn't eat of this tree"? By asking it as an indirect question, he tricked Eve into doing one of the most dangerous things you can do when you're in a relationship, and that is to discuss your private business with public sources. Eve's best response would have been not to entertain the conversation and realize she was not obligated to discuss anything about her private life.

Although people may not see you and your spouse out enjoying life publicly, it does not mean you are not both satisfied and happy in your private fun. Several chapters later, we can take a very interesting principle from the book of Genesis regarding the story of Noah and his sons. After his greatest success of obeying God, by building the ark, and providing shelter of safety for his family, he would also experience one of his greatest failures.

The Investment of Love

Genesis 9:20: And Noah began to be a farmer, and he planted a vineyard: **21**And he drank of the wine, and was drunken; and he was uncovered within his tent. **22**And Ham, the father of Canaan, saw the nakedness of his father, and told his two brothers without. **23**And Shem and Japheth took a garment, and laid it on both their shoulders, and went backward, and covered the nakedness of their father; and their faces were backward, and they saw not their father's nakedness.

The first thing to take away from this is that everyone can't handle you with your clothes off. Although Noah had a moment of transparency, the issue is that we have to be very careful of who sees us during private moments in our life. His son, Ham, couldn't handle seeing his father exposed and told others what he saw and experienced. However, the other two sons were able to perform damage control and didn't spread a rumor of their father having a human moment, but instead walked backward with a garment and covered him. The sons represent the types of people you have around you, those who will expose you, and those who will cover you.

I do not endorse the idea of getting drunk by any means. What I am saying is that in your moments of privacy, be careful of who you give access to your tent. Once close enough to you, they may not be able to handle everything they see or hear with discretion. Notice that Noah attempted to have some discretion with what he did by going into his tent. However, his son Ham was close enough to have the freedom of going into his father's personal space. James 5:16 tells us, "Confess *your* faults one to another, and pray one for another, that ye may be healed. The effectual fervent prayer of a righteous man availeth much." This scripture does not mean to find some random person and tell them everything about you. What it means is to confess your faults "one to another one of the same likeness."

Someone that is much like you can understand and provide a healthy level of counsel without standing in amazement of your issue or be in a hurry to break confidence in sharing it with other sources. A doctor would do no good confessing to a construction worker the problem he's having regarding a patient's diagnosis. They both are trained in two different areas and have no communication in common related to the same field of expertise. However, if a doctor approaches another doctor, he will not feel the fear of confiding in another doctor in fear of the exposure of having an issue.

The Investment of Love

Instead, it will be considered mentorship from a colleague who can offer advice and guidance.

Doctors have a reputation as "know it all's," not from their own opinions, but because of the power people have given them because of their platform. Many sports athletes and celebrities share this same curse of the crowd. This platform hinders their inability to be normal or common because their platforms cause people to view them as perfect or somehow above the normalcy of society. So, even though Doctors, Athletes, and Celebrities bleed red just like everyone else, it's a huge risk they take when trying to confess a fault, sin, or shortcoming with the average person. Their lives are always under the microscope filled with people ready to slam them from being imperfect. As it relates to the church, Pastors, Teachers, Apostles, Bishops, or Christians, in general, these titles and positions magnify the curse of the crowd effect times 10.

We have seen the many accounts in which public ministries have seen its fair share of private affairs and issues going public. Along with the backlash that comes with people being unforgiving towards those in ministry to have a second chance. By all means, yes! There is a standard in which we, as leaders and clergymen, must conduct ourselves. The crowd has created such a standard to hold leaders to, that even they are not willing to live.

Married Christian couples deserve to have a life just as anyone else does. You cannot rob yourself of a balanced healthy marriage because you're afraid of the standard people set for you. However, because of how people view us, we must have wisdom when conducting ourselves in the public view. You must develop a public front, but learn private fun. Now before you panic, at that statement, let's look at what a front is. The dictionary's definition of the word front is: the side or part of an object that presents itself to view or that is normally seen or used first; the most forward part of something. All of us have a side of that we normally and routinely show the public, and in turn, conceal a side of us for private use. This is just appropriate behavior for human nature and has been since the beginning of time. Popular culture and slang users have given the term front a negative connotation.

No matter how real or one hundred a person says they are, the truth of the matter is all of us are technically in some fashion, a front. Even if that front is as simple as the clothing, we wear in public to hide our nakedness, and although that is morally correct, it is still a front if you look at the truth of the matter. As Christian couples, you may have specific activities you like, things that set the mood for you, or places you go that provide a sense of emotional escape. As Christians, it doesn't mean you sit around and quote scriptures to each other all day, or listen to Gospel Music through times of intimacy. It is essential to understand this is not even the expectation of God for Christian Couples. If you desire to have a healthy relationship of any kind, there must be a balance.

What offends people doesn't mean it offends God, but we must use the wisdom of Romans 14:16, "Let not then your good be evil spoken of." I admonish you to read the entire chapter of Romans 14. Paul deals thoroughly with my aim of the chapter of this book. Just because we may be free in certain areas of our walk with Christ, doesn't mean others are. Meaning, we can't publicly do things that cause a setback to someone else's faith. Whatever is not done in faith is a sin to that individual. Although my wife has the faith and liberty of lipstick, makeup, and certain clothing doesn't mean everyone does. That being said, we are not to have that liberty in the presence of those who may not be on that level of relationship with God.

Paul says, "All things are lawful unto me, but all things are not expedient: all things are lawful for me, but I will not be brought under the power of any." Interpreting this is his way of saying everything is permissible to him, but not necessarily convenient and practical through the timing of doing it. Even the right thing around the wrong person can still be improper or immoral because it would cause more damage than good. To everything, there is a time and a season. The majority of being able to uphold your public reputation is based on knowing the proper time in which to do things. Even dinner dates with husbands and wives must be carefully planned with one another depending on the atmosphere you're going into, because even what we eat and drink can be offensive to others.

However, Paul even confirms and warns this as well in Romans 14:17-23: 17 For the kingdom of God is not a matter of eating and drinking, but of righteousness, peace and joy in the Holy Spirit, 18 because anyone who serves Christ in this way is pleasing to God and receives human approval. 19 Let us, therefore, make every effort to do what leads to peace and to mutual edification. 20 Do not destroy

The Investment of Love

the work of God for the sake of food. All food is clean, but it is wrong for a person to eat anything that causes someone else to stumble. **21** It is better not to eat meat or drink wine or to do anything else that will cause your brother or sister to fall. **22** So whatever you believe about these things keep between yourself and God. Blessed is the one who does not condemn himself by what he approves. **23** But whoever has doubts is condemned if they eat, because their eating is not from faith; and everything that does not come from faith is sin.

I can present the scripture, but I can't choose for you what to believe. Belief is based on your faith in God, which is based on your relationship with him. I can say though your guide towards your choices will be what you are or aren't feeling condemned about. I have so much discretion that I won't even write my stance on my beliefs regarding all my wife and myself choose to or not to enjoy. As verse 22 suggested, "This is to be kept between yourself and God." We are not to persuade people based on what we think but rather allow them the opportunity to have their own convictions and liberties based on their experiences, personal faith, and relationship with God.

www.ingramcontent.com/pod-product-compliance
Lightning Source LLC
Chambersburg PA
CBHW072252270326
41930CB00010B/2360